Change Is The Prelude

Developing trust in yourself and connecting with the part of you that knows what you really want out of life is transformational!

More than ever before, defining what it means to be fulfilled and living the life you want to be living is a personal challenge, one that you must meet on your own terms. This guided journal was designed to help you meet that challenge. Rather than listening to friends, colleagues, myths, media, and other influences that are all too ready to tell you what you should want, I want to encourage you to trust yourself, to ask yourself good questions, set realistic goals, remove fear and doubt and with every breath that you take move toward the goals that you have set for yourself and transformation will happen right before your eyes. Soon you will be living the life that you have envisioned for yourself.

When need and desire are greater than fear you will take the steps through your journey of change.

Your journey is personal and one of self-discovery. The process of journaling your journey will help you to better understand what you really want, how you really feel, and what may be the consequences of particular actions.

About The Author

Roslan is a Human Resources Professional and Business Consultant, Certified Executive and Life Coach, and Motivational Speaker. She is the Founder and Director of Bridging The Gap By Faith, a Non-profit Organization dedicated to the Spiritual, Physical, Emotional, Mental, and Economic Restoration and Empowerment of Women.

Roslan is a natural born coach, learning many of her skills from her mother, Rosie, the matriarch of the family that has coached so many in the realization of their greatest dreams. Through her mother's teachings, she learned and firmly believes that people typically have answers within themselves, but that they can sometimes use help in drawing those answers out. She believes that coaching should accelerate progress by providing focus and awareness. Coaching allows concentration on where you are now and what you are willing to do to get where you want to be in the future, recognizing that results are a matter of your intentions, choices and actions.

As a professional coach, Roslan has a deep understanding of human psychology and works with teams and individuals in such a way that inspires, empowers and motivates, raising self-esteem and increasing productivity. She has the ability to lead individuals to a place of high performance and excellence for achieving amazing results, through values-based goals, strategic planning, and heartfelt teamwork. She has over 20 years experience working with individuals and organizations in identifying performance gaps, recommending corrective action, creating and delivering training programs and providing one-on-one coaching for maximum results.

Roslan is the product of a many rich experiences that led her to graduate from Barclay Business College in 1985. She continued her education at CSULA, majoring in Psychology with a minor in Critical Thinking. She is currently pursuing the completion of a Masters Degree in Industrial Psychology with a concentration in Organizational Development.

Roslan has one adult son and one adult step-son and resides in the greater Los Angeles area. She is a member of a large and tremendously supportive family that is deeply rooted in their heritage, future and spirituality. God, Family, and her Sistas@Heart are first in her life and because of the close relationship she shares with her family she has opened her home and her heart to a number of family members and friends over the years.

Roslan has the gift of celebration and a passion for people and the events that shape their lives; marriage, birth, loss, celebrations, promotions and just plain everyday living. She attended CSULB to receive her certification in Event Design and Planning and is a Certified Meeting Planner, CMP. She has owned and operated Indelible Impressions, a full service Meeting and Event Planning Company for over ten years.

Roslan worked for a major airline for ten years and had the opportunity to travel and see the world. Travel is now a part of her DNA, tropical destinations are among her favorite places to visit.

<u>My</u> Journey in five stages by Roslan Monday

I.) <u>My</u> Present: Acknowledgment of My Current State.

II.) <u>My</u> Beliefs: I Believe I Can, I see me in the future doing what I want to do, being in the physical shape I want and surrounding myself with the things that will help me in my transformation.

III.) <u>My</u> Power: Connectivity and Oneness…this is the confirmation that I am connected, through the body of Christ, to an enormous family who has many resources that are there to aide me when I'm going through extraordinary transitions. It is this timeless wisdom that lets me know that even in my darkest hours, individually or collectively, I am never alone.

IV.) <u>My</u> Future: To align my passion with my goals and fulfill my destiny.

V.) <u>Maintenance</u>: I have had a lot of experience in the accomplishment of goals. My growth opportunity or change moment lies in maintenance. I have lost the same 50lbs at least five times in my adult life. Which is more powerful, to maintain the weight loss or to be able to lose it again? Of course I can lose it again, but if I learn to maintain, I can move on to the next goal.

Acknowledgment of my current state continues to be the most difficult part of my journey because just when I think I have all the answers, the questions change. That's life!! I am appreciative of the supportive friends and family members in my life because without them, this journey would have been derailed before it even started.

Today, I acknowledge that Life still has much to teach me and that I must approach each lesson with an open mind and a willingness to learn. As the Word of God says, "Be ye not conformed by the ways of this world but be ye transformed by the renewing of your mind that ye may prove what is that good, and acceptable, and perfect will of God".

"Transformed" is the Greek word "metamorphosis", meaning "an outer transformation due to an outworking of the inner nature".

My prayer is that you, my friends and family, are soon able to see the outward manifestation of the inward transformation going on with me every moment of my day and that you too can visualize me at the next phase in my journey.

I wish you Joy for your Journey as you create the "Change" that you want to see! I hope that you will come to view uncertainty as an opportunity and that you will know that Change is the prelude to Growth!

I dedicate this book to my mother, Rosie Monday, a meek woman who has dedicated her life to service for the Lord and her family. Matthew 5:5 Blessed are the meek: for they shall inherit the earth.

To my father, David Monday, who taught me that there really is victory over death in Christ Jesus. 1 Corinthians 15: 56-57 O death, where is thy sting? O grave, where Is thy victory? The sting of death is sin; and the strength of sin is the law. But thanks be to God, which giveth us the victory through our Lord Jesus Christ.

To my tremendously supportive family; T, Lee & BJ and the entire Monday, Griffin, Luckett and Stevens families have shown me that I am spiritually connected to the past, present and future. I am rich because of my heritage, because of the songs that I sing, the drums that I hear and the dance that is in my heart. I am not measured by the car that I drive, the job that I hold, or the home that I live in but by the values that I hold true, imparted to me by my family.

To Beverly, your support over these last several years has been a tremendous source of strength for me.

To Michelle, you have gone from the Valley to the Ocean and back with me a number of times; your selflessness will always be remembered.

To my Sistas@Heart who stand with me even when life has knocked me to my knees, your support over these 30 plus years could never be measured or duplicated.

To my son, Alance, who gives me great "Joy" and much to speak with God about while I'm on my knees.

To Antonio, one of "Life's" little lessons that has taught me that I can Stand, be Unmovable, Steadfast and always Abounding in the Work of The Lord, even in the midst of "Change".

Give your dreams wings.

Dream!

Let you heart be the guide.

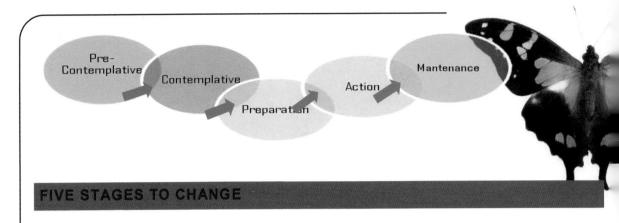

FIVE STAGES TO CHANGE

First there is *Precontemplation* – In this stage we are generally unaware of our problems or our current state and have no intention of changing our behavior. Why should we? We're quite contented with ourselves just as we are.

The second stage to change is *Contemplation* – In this stage we haven't yet made a commitment to take action, however, we acknowledge that something is wrong. If we suspect change will require some effort on our part; we remain hopeful that things will "automagically" improve on their own while we adjust to the current situation.

The third stage to change is *Preparation* – In this stage we intend to take action in the next few days. Now we are getting serious. We are not ready to detour from what is familiar and comfortable, but we are preparing ourselves for the new road and unchartered territory ahead and we are talking ourselves into the courage we will need if we're to actually explore what we must do in order to create change.

The fourth stage to change is *Action* – In this stage we finally take steps to overcome our problems. This is when we need all the courage we can drum up, because permanent change is not often easy —

The fifth and final stage to change is *Maintenance* – In this stage we work to consolidate our gains and prevent relapse. Maintenance is a lifetime of work.   It is important to remind ourselves that it took time to develop habits and beliefs — and it takes time to turn ourselves around until we're comfortable with the new person emerging from our work.

- ➢ What Motivates People to Change?
  - o When presented with clear and compelling information or awareness and conviction that the current "situation" is no longer working
- ➢ What prevents people from modifying behaviors?
  - o FEAR!! Fear of the Unknown
- ➢ Why Do YOU Want to Change?
  - o It is important to identify what you want to change and why because in the end, your motivation to change something about yourself may come from a variety of sources, perhaps because you are inspired by others to do something different, perhaps because of pain you may be experiencing as a consequence to a particular behavior or practice, perhaps you want to change because someone else thinks you should change. Being aware of your motivation to change is the best foundation upon which you begin to build your goals and plant the seed of change to set off on a new direction in life.

Here are some helpful tips:

1. Clearly state your objective and what it is you want to change.

_____

_____

_____

_____

2. Identify what motivates you to make that change and write it down.

_____

_____

_____

_____

Are you serious about changing your life? The questions below can help you discover who you are and where you want to go from this point forward.

No matter the goal, whether it is to lose 20 lbs or to meet and marry your soul mate, to achieve good health, live in abundance, or simply to have a better attitude, I believe that the questions below will help you discover how committed you are to change and how likely you are to achieve success and maintain the goal.

1. Am I willing to be totally honest with myself about myself and my opportunities for improvement?
Before you can become a different person, you have to start with who you are today. Acknowledging the areas of improvement opportunities that you have can help stop you from going around in circles and allow you to move forward.

_____

_____

_____

_____

So although you may want to transform some aspect of your life, character or habits and you may even be in the process of doing that, today it is what it is. To know what your current state of being and who you really are requires complete honesty. Otherwise you're wasting your time and energy.

2. What is true about me?
Once you decide you are willing to be honest with yourself, this question is much easier to answer. Without integrity, you will only see what you want to see, or what you think others would like you to be.

_____

_____

_____

_____

3. What is at the center of who I am and how can I strengthen this core of my being?

_____

_____

_____

_____

"Who you are" is not your bank account, the opinions you hold, the power or lack of power you exercise at work, or the relationships you have. The core of who you are is also not your body, your emotions, your actions, your ego, or your mind. Rather, it is something that people are searching for these days when we have increasing stress, pressures to conform and greed. Simply put, what makes you, you is your spirit. Your spirit can connect you with a power greater than yourself. Once the spirit is recognized and honored, it becomes the core /center of who you are and a place of comfort and deep resources you may not even be aware you possess.

This core, this center, this place of the spirit can help you counter the demands of the ego, such as the demand that you be perfect or that you are separate and better than those who are different from you or who don't see things the way you do.

Strengthening this core of your being will give you a refuge, a place to find peace from the piercing arrows of blame, shame and misfortune and everyday disappointments.

4. How did I get to where I am today?

_____

_____

_____

_____

It's not surprising you do what you do, say what you say, and think what you think. You were raised with different influences. While it isn't necessary to delve into your past in order to solve problems in the present, it helps to recognize that significant events in your life have left an impact. At the very least you should take a look at your history and this can help prevent you from repeating negative dynamics and passing them along to your children.

5. What are my strengths and what do I like about myself, others, my job, and about life in general?

_____

_____

_____

_____

It is not surprising that in times like these we can easily recognize our flaws, we have them, of course, but when you focus only on your faults, on the cracks in your relationships, on the body image that doesn't match the model's, on the aches and pains and chronic illness that are part of every life, your self-evaluation can become an obsession with imperfection.

When you acknowledge how special and unique you are despite your human imperfections or occasional lapse in judgment, you will have so much more to contribute to the world through your particular gifts.

In other words "Let it go……"

6. What would I like to have different in my life and is that possible?

_____

_____

_____

_____

If you aren't going anywhere in particular, any road you take will get you there. So be clear about your destination. Think about what it is you want to do and what it takes to make it happen. Are you willing to put in the work? Dream big, there is no dream too big that you can't have a starring role in it when it comes to life.

7. I've tried to achieve that objective before, what has stood in my way?

_____

_____

_____

_____

Don't be consumed by the reasons that it hasn't worked before but it is ok to explore how you can do things better, different the next time. As my Coach and Yoga instructor, Rochelle, told me, practice doesn't make perfect, it makes permanent!

We all have unconscious resistance to moving forward toward a solution that may take us into scary territory but when need and desire are greater than fear, you will move forward.

8. How does this goal relate to my other goals and does it enhance meaning and purpose in my life?

_____

_____

_____

_____

This question goes to the core of how you can sustain a sense of balance and harmony in your life when you're attempting to change something, especially if that something is a big self-improvement or relationship project. Change will, naturally, cause imbalance. That's the point!   Make sure that the changes you are going for are worth the energy and effort of changing your routine; make sure you are up for the challenge because when it works, life will not be the same.

So this question goes to the heart of choosing well the battles you want to fight. Why should you expend energy on an objective that isn't consistent with that which gives your life rich meaning and purpose? Are you following your dreams or someone else's?

9. What resources, tools or qualities would help me deal with this goal?

_____

_____

_____

_____

Certainly it is much easier to tackle problems, both small and large, when you have at your disposal the whole array of resources and qualities of the human spirit. For some goals you may need patience, for others assertiveness. In some cases compassion and forgiveness are needed, in others, joy and creativity.

10. What image or symbol can reinforce or support my intention to change?

_____

_____

_____

_____

I choose the butterfly. Why the butterfly? Because the butterfly just sees change as the next step. In its caterpillar stage, it creates its little cocoon, goes inside, and when times up, and after quite a work out, it emerges, transformed into a butterfly. It stretches its newfound wings and flies away to discover new things in life! Yes, it is time for the caterpillar to give life to the butterfly.

Find a symbol that you identify with and that supports your change.

11. What small step am I willing to take to move toward my goal?

_____

_____

_____

_____

Every transformation, just like every ripple, has a point of origin. Consider the effect of your thoughts and actions, and how they move you toward your goal. Rather than becoming overwhelmed by the enormity of the goal you've decided to set for yourself take one small step at a time. Explore how to take minor, do-able steps from intention to achievement.

_____

_____

_____

_____

_____

_____

_____

_____

_____

_____

_____

ACKNOWLEDGMENT!

Do you have a dream?

Do you have a problem you need to solve?

Do you have a relationship that needs healing?

Do you have a job that needs to be done?

Do you want your life to be better, easier and more satisfying than it is today?

Stop wishing your life was different; use these blank pages to make it happen. Set goals, work towards those goals and sustain the changes once you have achieved them.

Know Who You Are

- ➤ WHO AM I?: Define yourself as an individual, separate from all others

    - o You are not the child, spouse or parent but just "You". Who Are You?

- ➤

    WHAT MAKES ME SPECIAL?: Know how special you are

    - o Are you a poet, a designer, an artist, a baker, a candle maker? What are your passions and your causes? Do you live out loud and in color?

IS THERE A PATTERN TO MY LIFE? Have you been here before? Step out of the comfort zone and do something different, shake things up a little. That's it, shock your system!

Write the first five descriptive words that come to mind to define yourself and journal why those words describe you. If the words that you choose are negative, ask yourself why, and work on changing how that word describes you. Repeat this exercise quarterly, the goal of this exercise is to replace the negative thoughts with the power of positive thoughts and praise.

_____

_____

_____

_____

_____

_____

WHAT ARE MY GIFTS?: Find and pursue your passions

WHO CAN I TRUST?: Remove the "dream-killers" from your inner-circle and surround yourself with positive progressive people.

WHAT IS MY MESSAGE?: Define for yourself what matters to you

Recognize your gifts and talents…are you living your dream, following your passion or are you afraid to step out and use your gifts to make your living and to bless the world?

_____

_____

_____

_____

_____

_____

_____

_____

_____

_____

_____

_____

_____

_____

Don't let your problems and tough times get you down. Harness the power of positive thinking. One of the most powerful forces in this world is the power of positive thinking. Our circumstances or conditions do not determine what our lives become nearly as much as the thoughts that dominate our minds. No one can ever overcome anything until their thoughts are creative and positive.

Mentally, as you raise your mind above the conflicts you face, your personality "Spirit" will receive help from God in the form of clear thinking, resolute reaching out toward happiness, deeper understanding and renewed strength. When your thoughts are in confusion or you feel depressed, you live in an unreal world, you cannot see your way out.

Here are some ways you can replace confusion and depression with the courage and insight to face your problems and overcome them.

1. Monitor your moods.
For instance, you go to your doctor for a healthy check up and when the nurse takes your blood pressure, it is elevated so she notes your file and asks you a few questions, compares it to your history of blood pressure readings and reminds you to come back if you have any symptoms of blood pressure disease. The next time you come in for the blood pressure reading it is within your normal range, again the nurse notes your file, asks you a few questions, reminds you to call if you have any symptoms related to blood pressure disease but she does not have any alarm. Predictably, when the reading is too high and stays high for a period of time, people get concerned and the results should be monitored.

Everything moves according to a rhythm. This is true not only for the rotation of the earth, the diastolic and systolic flow of your blood pressure, but also of human moods. It is not necessary to be overly concerned when your mood drops a little; that's normal. Nor need you be overly elated when your mood rises. That, too, is normal. Your consideration and focus should be when your mood goes down and stays down. That's when you need to seek help; you need an answer to the question, "How can I lift my spirit?"

2. Think of the sun.
When you're discouraged, despairing, or in a time of darkness, never forget that the sun will ultimately shine again; its absence is never permanent. Hang on to your faith; know that soon you will rise into the light again. One of my dearest friends, Katrina, always tells me that the sun is shining even when I can't see it.

A wise woman, Michelle, another dear friend of mine, once told me, "The human spirit perishes without the sun". So on those spiritually overcast, cloudy days, make your own sunlight. Create it in your heart, let it radiate from the tip of your head to the souls of your feet and soon you will feel it warming your bones, entering into the essence of your being. You can do this by thinking of the things that warm your spirit and make you smile. Go ahead, write them down!!

_____

_____

_____

_____

Nothing can happen in life that is so bad that the sun will not shine again. Remember all the good things that God has done for you in the past. That is the sunlight of the past. Then visualize—and never let the visualization become dim—the sunlight of the future, all the good that God will do for you and your loved ones in the future. Always remember the sunlight of the past, and the sunlight of the future, in the dark days.

3. Clear your mind.

Another way to lift your spirit is to empty your mind of all negative thoughts—all hateful, apprehensive and fearful thoughts. Note how much better you feel, how your spirit is lifted. You can hardly expect your spirit to soar, when it is weighed down with resentment, self-pity and ill will. If you carry negative thoughts, your spirit is held down. Don't replay the tapes of the past like a scratched CD or DVD where it skips over and over and over again constantly repeating, like a mantra, your self-pity and fears.

So what to do? Breathe and Meditate, lift up your eyes to the high places, "The Hills From Which Cometh Your Help, Your Help Comes From God". Get your mind off destructive attitudes toward other people. Get your mind off yourself, your failures and resentments. Look fearlessly at all the gloom and remind yourself that it is not permanent. "This too shall pass." We must lift up our minds to God and let faith pour down into us. Then our spirits will rise like the wings of an Eagle and our souls will soar high, all our days.

Positive Affirmation
A) Remember all the good God has done for you in the past; visualize all the good God will do for you in the future.
B) Make a conscious choice to feed yourself with positivity.

As you become increasingly comfortable with being yourself, your heart overflows with joy. Take a moment now to experience love flowing throughout your body, filling every pore and extending to others.

+ Retire Your Representative and just be "Your True Self". Do others see the real you or do you send the representative you think others want to see?

How does it feel to just be you?

_____

_____

_____

_____

_____

_____

_____

_____

_____

_____

_____

_____

_____

_____

_____

_____

_____

_____

_____

Know that "You" are good enough, just as you are. Know how special you are.

Round And Around In Circles....

De Ja Vu...do you ever experience it? Have you been here before? Is it the same thing just a different day, year, place and even people but the same old thing? Is the situation and the people involved different, yet one experience after the other, it feels exactly like the last one and the one before that one?

Perhaps you had a really bad neighbor when you lived in the old house and now that you have moved you find yourself experiencing similar challenges with your new neighbors. Does your relationship with a new romantic partner seem a lot like your old relationship with your old partner and the problems seem to be the same? You may feel disappointed or frustrated and wonder why the same situations and people keep showing up in your life. The truth is that the same kinds of experiences don't keep happening to us. After all, the circumstances and the people involved are always different. The truth is, we keep experiencing things the same way or having the same experience because we haven't changed. This is kind of like trying ten different diets and having the same results. The Change begins with us!

Perhaps there is something to be said for having the same experiences in life until we are ready to have a different experience. It begins with us and how we feel about ourselves or how we compare ourselves to others. Maybe you feel unworthy of happiness, or worry that your race or skin color will get in the way of your success. Maybe you believe that others see your hair as too kinky or too straight, or are afraid that your braids won't work in Corporate America. Maybe you believe, because of images and values that you've bought into, that you are too tall or too short, too thick or too thin to have the relationship that you desire or the promotion that you've earned. Do you unknowingly hold yourself back because of how you think others perceive you? Are you making their issues your own? Are you putting yourself in a box? ...get out of that box that's Jack's house!

Our experiences tend to reflect what we believe about life. After all, most of us don't like to be proven wrong. We may even experience a sense of satisfaction in being right or experience a sense of safety every time we confirm to ourselves that we know the way the world works.

We may choose a relationship partner who is very different from our last partner and hope that this time love will turn out differently. Yet as long as we hold whatever beliefs we have and repeat the same mistakes, we will continue to limit the good we can experience and we will create the same dynamic of limited happiness in our life.

Again, the key to turning this situation around is *YOU*. You can *CHANGE* your experience by changing your perception of yourself, your expectations, your beliefs and your limitations.

Change the language that you use, be inclusive and positive. Change your thoughts. Our thoughts become our words and our words become our actions. Change your associations. Ensure that you are with positive, progressive, forward thinking individuals that share some of the same goals and life philosophies that you hold. Change your acceptance of everybody and everything as a part of the inner-circle of your life. You don't have to judge but you don't have to compromise your standards either. You can choose what you will accept and who you will affiliate with. "If it don't fit, don't force it!" Change begins with you. Identify for yourself who you are and what you want from your life. Some of these experiences will have to change because you have redefined who you are and what your expectations will be for every situation, whether it be a romantic relationship, family, friends, work or social.

We bring ourselves and our beliefs into every situation. If we can figure out which of our beliefs are no longer serving us, we can consciously change those beliefs, make new choices, and start having new kinds of experiences that are in line with what we want in life.

CHANGE is within your reach and your power! Make it your goal. I know, you are asking exactly how do you make this change. Well the pages to follow are the pages reflective of your personal journey of change. Now that you've acknowledged your present, and you can envision your future, all that is left to do is identify the goals and develop a process. A process is a procedure or a particular course of action intended to achieve a result.

What beliefs or values have you bought into that are not serving you well and are holding your back?

_____

_____

_____

_____

_____

_____

_____

_____

PREPARATION FOR THE DAY AHEAD

How do you prepare for the day? When you awaken, do you spend time alone, do you breath, stretch, mediate and put on your armor? Or do you rush right out to engage with the world?

Spending time alone will prepare you for the day ahead and will allow you to clearly focus on you, your goals, your needs and God's plan for your life.

First: Spend some time thanking God for all that he has already done and all that he will do in the future.

Second: Meditate on God's Word, choose a scripture to read and allow yourself some time to meditate on this scripture and how to apply it in your daily activity.

Third: Breathe! Sit back comfortably, if standing is your only option, let your arms drop easily at your side, stand with your feet slightly apart and see if you feel balanced and okay on your feet. Take several breaths all the way in and all the way out. Let your body relax and feel your shoulders and hands relaxing, feel the trunk of your body relaxed and centered. Breathe deep and let your body relax, let go for 2-5 minutes, longer if you can. Now you have bought your"Self"' some breathing room and believe it or not, you did the same for the next person, place or thing you interact with.

Finally: Get dressed by putting on the whole armor of God that you may be able to stand against the wiles of the devil. For we do not wrestle against flesh and blood, but against principalities, against powers, against the rulers of the darkness of this age, against spiritual hosts of wickedness in the heavenly places.

Now you are prepared to take the day head on!

Calm your mind & nourish your soul

Acknowledge the present moment
Take time to say goodbye to life as it was
Trust in the process and your inner wisdom to guide you
Allow life to unfold as you make space for passion & meaning to emerge
Fredda Wesserman

PROCESS:

Letting Go of Fear: When need and desire are greater than fear, we move forward.

Write your fears out in this journal. By writing these thoughts down, they are no longer a part of you.

_____

_____

_____

_____

After writing out your fears then answer several questions:

What can I learn from these fears?

_____

_____

What can I change?

_____

_____

What can I surrender?

_____

_____

What are five blessings in my life?

_____

_____

By answering these questions you have shifted your thoughts from fear to insight and gratitude.

Empowering Tools To Help Overcome Fear

- Pray

The Serenity Prayer is very powerful: God grant me the serenity to accept the things I cannot change, the courage to change those that I can, and the wisdom to know the difference.

First, God grant me the serenity to accept the things I cannot change. This is recognition that "Change" is constant and nothing stays the same. We must accept that our freedom of choice is being challenged and limitations are being placed on our decisions. We must accept that the things we once took for granted, the economy, our jobs, security, our habits and the things we knew for sure are changing. God grant me the serenity to accept the things I cannot change, means being able to surrender those things that are out of our control over to God. Surrender is a process and can be accomplished through prayer, meditation, imagery, visualization, and journaling your feelings. The courage to know the difference - refers to qualities of spirit and conduct that allows you to face extreme dangers, difficulties, disappointment and challenges without fear.

- Meditate

Meditation is the ability to quiet down the mind, body and spirit. A simple way to begin is to find a quiet spot where you won't be disturbed. Sit, stand or lie down. Close your eyes. Take a deep breath in through your nose and feel the breath travel down into your belly. Visualize a white healing light. White light is the space within the universe where positive energies are stored. White light can be called upon by anyone (healers, empaths, and you too!) for protection from negative energies.

Take a deep cleansing inhale through your nose, feel the breath fill up the cavity of your lungs and travel through your body, feel it at the tips of your fingers and down to your toes, hold the breath for several seconds now exhale through your mouth, audibly.

Repeat this several times until you can feel your body relaxing. When you are in this relaxed state, imagine yourself filling up a large hot air balloon, placing all of your fears in the hot air balloon, and then release your fear-filled balloon to the universe. Once you have released your fear, visualize the highest outcome for any situation you are fearful of.

- Spend time in nature
  Nature has a wonderfully calming effect on the body, mind, and spirit. When you are feeling fearful take a walk on the beach, through the park or on a mountain trail, you will connect with nature and fear and anxiety will flee.

- Listen to beautiful music
  Listen to whatever music soothes your soul. For me it is smooth Jazz, for you it could be R&B, Hip-Hop, Classical Jazz or Mediation but you will find that your blues will be chased away by the sound of the music.

- Read uplifting inspiring books
  Fearful thoughts can be soothed by inspirational reading material with topics such as… Spirituality, Motivation and Personal growth.

- Seek out positive people
  Many of our friends may be experiencing anxieties of their own, if this is the case for your friends and they are feeling fearful right now, seek out new friends and social groups for some spiritually, uplifting events.   Try a local Church group; book club; volunteer groups; Network groups and Community groups as they frequently have uplifting events and opportunities for you to network and socialize with and to give back to the community or a cause. This is a gift that gives you something back!

If you are still experiencing fear after implementing these strategies seek the assistance of a professional that can help you walk through your fears. Minister, Behavioral Psychologist, EAP, Spiritual or Life Coach, and Meditation guides are professionals that can empower you with tools to help you let go of your fear.

- Savor every moment in your life
  Don't wait for the next big holiday, experience or birthday to celebrate. Enjoying, celebrating and living life in the moment is perhaps most important element in eliminating fear. None of us know what tomorrow brings, God's Word says for us to not be anxious for tomorrow for each day has its own badness, loosely translated, today has enough for us to

concern ourselves with, live in this moment and tomorrow will take care of itself. Everyday make time to tell the people in your life that you love them, watch a sun set, listen to the birds singing and give thanks for every breath that you take!

 Although we are living in evolving times, the power of our thoughts, intentions, and actions can greatly affect the outcome of our lives. By implementing some of these strategies you can learn to let go of fear and begin to live your life fully again.

Simply stated, we create the world we live in by our thoughts and beliefs. Our experiences shape the way we think and the way we think shape our experiences. Once our thoughts and our actions are in alignment with our values and our goals, our experiences will be more aligned with our expectations.

Your Journey Through Change Begins With You

The future you envision is waiting for you, if you can dream it, you can live it. Use these blank pages to start your process and claim the life you want.

Refuse to be satisfied with mediocrity and never become contented with the status quo. Challenge yourself to strive for improvement on an ongoing basis by holding out an ideal of personal wholeness and integration as the ultimate horizon of growth while recognizing that development and growth require time and sustained effort.

It really doesn't matter if you take baby steps or really big giant steps, what is important is that you just take steps!

Step off of the rollercoaster that just goes round and round and has no end, spinning out of control without any accomplishment.

The activity steps help you to see clearly your greatest dreams, desires and goals and can help you develop a plan or process to achieve these things.

The pages ahead are mostly blank; they will be as colorful and as useful as you create them. They reflect your goals and your dreams and the steps that you are willing to take to achieve these goals.

Let's go…

You may have many goals so repeat this process as many times as you need to with different goals or the same goal. The key here is to create a plan, a process to identify your goals and a way to achieve them. Personal goal setting is the wisdom that comes out of previous experience and should help you direct your conscious and subconscious actions towards success, building up your motivation to achieve your personal or business goals.

GOAL:

Can you visualize the desired outcome(s)? How will you know if you have reached the goal? How will you measure success? What limitations do you have such as insufficient time, insufficient money or investors, dependence on other people or other resources?

_____

_____

_____

_____

_____

_____

_____

_____

_____

_____

Actions:

Write down all actions you may need to take to achieve your goal. At this step focus on generating and writing as many different options and ideas as possible. Write more and more ideas, just as they come to your mind. While you are doing this, try not to judge or analyze.

_____

_____

_____

_____

_____

_____

_____

_____

_____

_____

_____

_____

_____

_____

_____

_____

_____

_____

Analyze, prioritize, and delete.

Look at your list of actions. What are the absolutely necessary and effective steps to achieve your goal? Make a list of those steps. After that, what action items can be dropped from the plan without significant consequences for the outcome? Cross them out.

_____

_____

_____

_____

_____

_____

_____

_____

_____

_____

_____

_____

_____

_____

_____

_____

_____

_____

Organize:

Decide on the order of your action steps. Start from looking at your key actions. For each action, what other steps should be completed before that action? Rearrange your actions and ideas into a sequence of ordered action steps. Finally, look at your plan once again. Are there any ways to simplify it even more?

_____

_____

_____

_____

_____

_____

_____

_____

_____

_____

_____

_____

_____

_____

_____

_____

_____

Monitor your steps and process regularly, review and revise your plan as necessary:

How much have you progressed towards your goal by now? What new information do you have? Use this information to further adjust and optimize your plan.

_____

_____

_____

_____

_____

_____

_____

_____

_____

_____

_____

_____

_____

_____

_____

_____

_____

How will you benefit from achieving this goal? If you are not sure of the benefits you may find it difficult to maintain the necessary persistence, dedication and enthusiasm!

_____

_____

_____

_____

_____

_____

_____

_____

_____

_____

_____

_____

_____

_____

_____

_____

_____

_____

_____

Progress Check: Goal _____

What have been your successes towards this goal?

_____

_____

_____

_____

1) What challenges have you discovered?

_____

_____

_____

_____

2) What new opportunities did you discover during this process?

_____

_____

_____

_____

3) What additional resources might help you?

_____

_____

_____

_____

_____

_____

Progress Check: Goal _____

What have been your successes towards this goal?

_____

_____

_____

_____

1) What challenges have you discovered?

_____

_____

_____

_____

2) What new opportunities did you discover during this process?

_____

_____

_____

_____

3) What additional resources might help you?

_____

_____

_____

_____

Progress Check: Goal _____

What have been your successes towards this goal?

_____

_____

_____

_____

1) What challenges have you discovered?

_____

_____

_____

_____

2) What new opportunities did you discover during this process?

_____

_____

_____

_____

3) What additional resources might help you?

_____

_____

_____

_____

Progress Check: Goal _____

What have been your successes towards this goal?

_____
_____
_____
_____

   1) What challenges have you discovered?

_____
_____
_____
_____

   2) What new opportunities did you discover during this process?

_____
_____
_____
_____

   3) What additional resources might help you?

_____
_____
_____
_____

Progress Check: Goal _____

What have been your successes towards this goal?

_____

_____

_____

_____

1) What challenges have you discovered?

_____

_____

_____

_____

2) What new opportunities did you discover during this process?

_____

_____

_____

_____

3) What additional resources might help you?

_____

_____

_____

_____

_____

Progress Check: Goal _____

What have been your successes towards this goal?

_____

_____

_____

_____

1) What challenges have you discovered?

_____

_____

_____

_____

2) What new opportunities did you discover during this process?

_____

_____

_____

_____

3) What additional resources might help you?

_____

_____

_____

_____

Progress Check: Goal _____

What have been your successes towards this goal?

_____

_____

_____

_____

1) What challenges have you discovered?

_____

_____

_____

_____

2) What new opportunities did you discover during this process?

_____

_____

_____

_____

3) What additional resources might help you?

_____

_____

_____

_____

Progress Check: Goal _____

What have been your successes towards this goal?

_____

_____

_____

_____

    1)   What challenges have you discovered?

_____

_____

_____

_____

    2)   What new opportunities did you discover during this process?

_____

_____

_____

_____

    3)   What additional resources might help you?

_____

_____

_____

_____

Maintenance:

Now that you have achieved your goals, what now? How do you maintain the achievement? What do you do next?

There are various strategies for maintaining the goal once you have achieved a milestone.

1. Set a new (bigger) goal. This works well in areas where there is room for expansion. The goal is to never become complacent or happy with the status quo. Never stop dreaming, never settle for the path that is least resistant, and keep experiencing new and exciting things in life.
2. Expand on the first goals that you set, perhaps if your goal was to lose weight and get in shape to become a healthier happier you, now you may want to get a certification to teach the principles that made you successful at attaining this goal.
3. Sharpen your skills in a new area, in our ever changing world, you will find just as you think you have all the answers, the questions have just changed. Life-long learning, life-long sharing, and life-long loving will help you maintain and achieve new goals. Go ahead; repeat the process for all of your new goals!

_____

_____

_____

_____

_____

_____

_____

_____

Progress Check: Goal _____

What have been your successes towards this goal?

_____

_____

_____

_____

1) What challenges have you discovered?

_____

_____

_____

_____

2) What new opportunities did you discover during this process?

_____

_____

_____

_____

3) What additional resources might help you?

_____

_____

_____

_____

Progress Check: Goal _____

What have been your successes towards this goal?

_____

_____

_____

_____

    4)   What challenges have you discovered?

_____

_____

_____

_____

    5)   What new opportunities did you discover during this process?

_____

_____

_____

_____

    6)   What additional resources might help you?

_____

_____

_____

_____

Progress Check: Goal _____

What have been your successes towards this goal?

_____

_____

_____

_____

1) What challenges have you discovered?

_____

_____

_____

_____

2) What new opportunities did you discover during this process?

_____

_____

_____

_____

3) What additional resources might help you?

_____

_____

_____

_____

Progress Check: Goal _____

What have been your successes towards this goal?

_____

_____

_____

_____

1) What challenges have you discovered?

_____

_____

_____

_____

2) What new opportunities did you discover during this process?

_____

_____

_____

_____

3) What additional resources might help you?

_____

_____

_____

_____

Progress Check: Goal _____

What have been your successes towards this goal?

_____

_____

_____

_____

   1)   What challenges have you discovered?

_____

_____

_____

_____

   2)   What new opportunities did you discover during this process?

_____

_____

_____

_____

   3)   What additional resources might help you?

_____

_____

_____

_____

Progress Check: Goal _____

What have been your successes towards this goal?

_____

_____

_____

_____

1) What challenges have you discovered?

_____

_____

_____

_____

2) What new opportunities did you discover during this process?

_____

_____

_____

_____

3) What additional resources might help you?

_____

_____

_____

_____

Progress Check: Goal _____

What have been your successes towards this goal?

_____

_____

_____

_____

1) What challenges have you discovered?

_____

_____

_____

_____

2) What new opportunities did you discover during this process?

_____

_____

_____

_____

3) What additional resources might help you?

_____

_____

_____

_____

Progress Check: Goal _____

What have been your successes towards this goal?

_____

_____

_____

_____

1) What challenges have you discovered?

_____

_____

_____

_____

2) What new opportunities did you discover during this process?

_____

_____

_____

_____

3) What additional resources might help you?

_____

_____

_____

_____

Made in the USA